My New Pet

Hamster and Gerbil

Jinny Johnson

W
FRANKLIN WATTS
LONDON•SYDNEY

An Appleseed Editions book

Paperback edition 2015

First published in 2013 by Franklin Watts
338 Euston Road, London NW1 3BH

Franklin Watts Australia
Hachette Children's Books
Level 17/207 Kent St, Sydney, NSW 2000

© 2013 Appleseed Editions

Created by Appleseed Editions Ltd,
Well House, Friars Hill, Guestling,
East Sussex TN35 4ET

Designed by Guy Callaby
Edited by Mary-Jane Wilkins
Illustrations by Bill Donohoe

ISBN 978 1 4451 3845 9

Dewey Classification 636.9'356

Contents

 I'm very excited. My mum says I can have a hamster. My brother is going to have a gerbil.

We want to know all about hamsters and gerbils so we can look after our pets well.

Here's what we've found out.

Hamsters make great pets and they are easy to look after.

Pet hamsters usually live for two to three years.

A hamster is a **rodent** (like rats and mice). It has short legs and a tiny tail.

Wild hamsters sleep during the day. Pet hamsters sleep during the day, too. They wake up to eat and play in the evening.

You can keep different types of hamsters as pets. **Syrian** hamsters are the most popular and they like to live by themselves. They fight if you keep them in pairs.

Russian or dwarf hamsters like company, so you can keep two together. Chinese hamsters have a longer tail.

*Don't keep a boy and girl Russian hamster together or you will end up with lots of **babies**.*

We'll look for a Syrian hamster with bright **eyes** and a smooth, glossy **coat**. We will check its tail area and make sure it is clean.

We will buy a big **wire** cage with a plastic base.

*A **tank-style** cage is best for dwarf hamsters.*

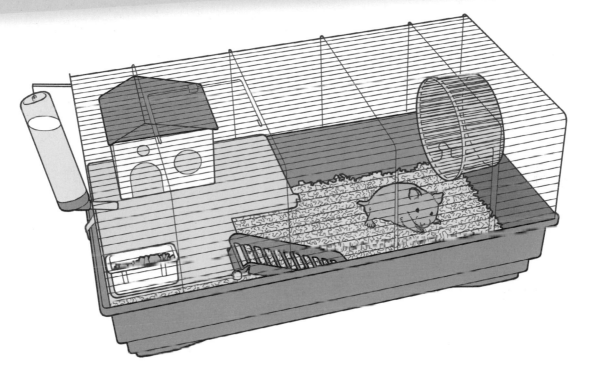

Wood shavings will soak up the hamster's wee. Hamsters like to burrow, so we will put some **shredded paper** or **peat** in the cage, too.

I know my hamster will be **nervous** at first so I will let it get used to its new home. After the first few days I will let it sniff my hand and then pick it up gently.

Hamsters spend a lot of time grooming to keep their fur clean.

I will feed my pet dried food for hamsters.  I will give it some fresh food, such as **carrot** and **apple**, and change its drinking water every day.

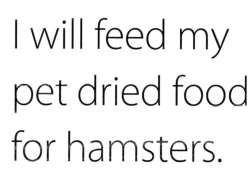

Gerbils are gentle little animals and fun to keep as pets. They are rodents (like rats and mice) and they have sharp **teeth** and a long hairy **tail**.

Pet gerbils live for between two and four years.

Gerbils live in groups in the wild, so it's best to have two or three. Don't keep **males** and **females** together, or they will have lots of babies.

13

Baby gerbils are usually ready to leave their mum when they are about five or six weeks old. Pet shops often sell **Mongolian** gerbils. with brown, grey, golden, cream or black coats.

Gerbils play together and groom each other, which is fun to watch.

We want a bright, lively gerbil with a clean **nose** and **eyes**, and a glossy **coat**.

A pair of gerbils needs a big cage: at least 40 x 75 x 30 cm. Our pets will be happiest if they can **dig** and **tunnel** in their cage.

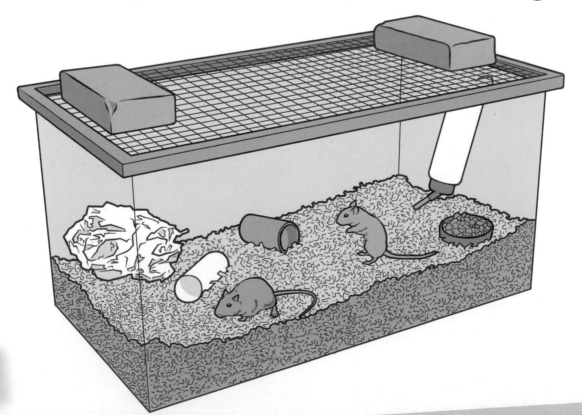

They need **wood shavings** to burrow in and some shredded **paper** for nesting. Gerbils also like a layer of **peat** to dig in.

Gerbils often say hello to each other by touching noses.

We will give our gerbils dried and fresh food every day. Apples, carrots, broccoli and cauliflower are all good. They need fresh water every day, too.

We will be very gentle when picking up the gerbils and won't grab them. We must never squeeze and never pick them up by the tail.

Gerbils are **active** all day and all night. They sleep for a few hours, wake up for a while, then take another nap.

Hamsters and gerbils need our help to keep their cages tidy.

We'll **check** their cages every day and take out uneaten food.

Every week we'll put them in a **safe** place and wash and dry their cages. Then we'll put in fresh bedding.

Hamsters and gerbils enjoy time out of their cage, but we 'll keep them on the **floor** so they can't fall and hurt themselves.

Notes for parents

Choosing a pet
Make sure you buy healthy hamsters or gerbils from a good pet shop or breeder. Take the animals to the vet for a health check. Ask the vet to check the sex of the animals too. Pet shops sometimes get it wrong!

Handling and caring for small animals
Show children how to handle animals properly. Teach them to respect their pets and always treat them gently.

Health
As a parent you need to make sure that any pet is looked after properly. Supervise feeding and handling, especially at first. Check regularly for signs of parasites and take your pets to the vet if they show signs of illness.

Words to remember

grooming
Cleaning the fur.

parasites
Tiny creatures such as fleas, lice and mites, which can live on a hamster's or gerbil's body.

rodents
A group of mammals that includes rats and mice, as well as hamsters and gerbils.

Index